The Chartered Financial Analyst® Program

CFA® Level I
Half-way There Mock Examination

2014

Your Half-way There Mock Examination Exam consists of 120 multiple choice questions which must be completed in three hours. The topic areas covered are:

BPP
LEARNING MEDIA

Published January 2014

ISBN 978 1 4727 0414 6

eISBN 9781 4727 0438 2

British Library Cataloguing-in-Publication Data
A catalogue record for this book is available from the British Library

Published by

BPP Learning Media Ltd
BPP House, Aldine Place
142-144 Uxbridge Road
London W12 8AA

www.bpp.com/learningmedia

Printed in United Kingdom by Ricoh
Ricoh House, Ullswater Cresent
Coulsdon CR5 2HR

Your learning materials, published by BPP Learning Media Ltd, are printed on paper obtained from traceable, sustainable sources.

A note about copyright

Dear Customer

What does the little © mean and why does it matter? Your market-leading BPP books, course materials and e-learning materials do not write and update themselves. People write them: on their own behalf or as employees of an organisation that invests in this activity. Copyright law protects their livelihoods. It does so by creating rights over the use of the content.

Breach of copyright is a form of theft – as well being a criminal offence in some jurisdictions, it is potentially a serious breach of professional ethics.

With current technology, things might seem a bit hazy but, basically, without the express permission of BPP Learning Media:

- Photocopying our materials is a breach of copyright
- Scanning, ripcasting or conversion of our digital materials into different file formats, uploading them to facebook or emailing them to your friends is a breach of copyright

You can, of course, sell your books, in the form in which you have brought them – once you have finished with them. (Is this fair to your fellow students? We update for a reason.)

And what about outside the UK? BPP Learning Media strives to make our materials available at prices students can afford by local printing arrangements, pricing policies and partnerships which are clearly listed on our website. A tiny minority ignore this and indulge in criminal activity by illegally photocopying our material or supporting organisations that do. If they act illegally and unethically in one area, can you really trust them?

BPP
LEARNING MEDIA

Ethical and Professional Standards

1. Which one of the following is *least likely* to justify a CFA Institute member from breaching the confidentiality of information received from a client?

    A. The information is material and non-public.

    B. The information relates to another member's misconduct under investigation by CFA Institute's Professional Conduct Program.

    C. The member receives the information on the basis of his special ability to conduct a portion of the client's affairs.

2. Which one of the following is *least likely* to be an objective of the Global Investment Performance Standards (GIPS®)?

    A. Fair global competition among firms.

    B. To encourage global regulation of performance standards by CFA Institute.

    C. Worldwide acceptance of a standard for calculation and presentation of results in a fair and comparable manner.

3. John Jones CFA works for ABC Investment Advisers, which provides investment advice to a hospital endowment fund. Jones receives confidential information from the trustees of the endowment concerning its affairs. Jones receives a request from a doctor in the hospital to receive the information to solicit money from a rich potential donor.

    Which of the following courses of action is *most appropriate* to be in compliance with the Code of Ethics and Standards of Professional Conduct?

    A. Jones may not release the information to the doctor.

    B. Jones may release the information because the doctor's actions are designed to benefit the endowment fund.

    C. Jones may release the information so long as he subsequently informs the trustees of the endowment that he has done so.

4. Which of the following best describes the 'mosaic theory'?

    A. An analyst who is a CFA member is required to have knowledge of the mosaic of international laws appropriate to his area of expertise.

    B. An analyst is guilty of insider trading if he receives a mosaic of material nonpublic information from an insider to a company.

    C. An analyst is not guilty of insider trading if he builds up a mosaic of information, each part of which is non material nonpublic information in itself but which taken together could be seen as material, and acts on this mosaic of information.

5. Which of the following is the best description of the requirements under the Code of Ethics and Standards of Professional Conduct in respect of a supervisor who is a CFA charterholder planning to delegate supervisory duties to junior staff, some of whom are candidates in the CFA program but some of whom have no responsibility under the Standards?

   A. The supervisor does not have responsibility where the supervisory duties have been delegated.

   B. The supervisor retains responsibility in respect of all the junior staff.

   C. The supervisor does not have responsibility for junior employees not subject to CFA Institute Standards.

6. Which of the following is *most likely* in breach of Standard III.A – Loyalty, Prudence and Care?

   A. Jo Investment Management uses soft dollar practices.

   B. Ken Investment Management votes proxies on nonroutine matters but not on routine matters.

   C. Jonty Investment Management directs brokerage to particular brokers in response to requests of the clients concerned.

7. Lisa Sparrow CFA works for Wilkinson Investment Company, which specializes in funds with long-term investment objectives. Recently, a large number of employees left the firm to set up their own company and, in order to retain Sparrow's services, Wilkinson has put into place a new bonus scheme based on her performance over the next six months. Sparrow does not inform her clients of the change in her compensation arrangement. Which of the following statements is *most accurate*?

   A. Sparrow has not breached the Standards unless she allows the change in compensation arrangement to affect her investment decisions.

   B. Sparrow has breached the Standards by accepting the compensation arrangement.

   C. Sparrow has breached the Standards by not informing her clients of the change in compensation arrangements.

8. Kurt Wilson is due to visit the headquarters of Won Industries to find out information that he hopes to be able to use in his research report. Won offers to pay for Wilson's trip, including his meals, airfare and hotel bills. Which of the following is *the best course* of action for Kurt to take in order to avoid breaching the Standards?

   A. Accept the expenses-paid trip, but ensure that the report that he writes is objective.

   B. Accept the expenses-paid trip, but disclose the benefits received and ensure that he is able to return the favor.

   C. Visit the headquarters, but pay for all the expenses himself.

9. John Parrot passed Level I of the CFA examinations last year. He intends to register to sit Level II next year. Janet Lynam has passed Level III and been awarded the CFA charter. Parrot refers to himself as a CFA candidate on his CV and stresses that this does not represent a partial designation and that he will register to set the Level II exam at the scheduled sitting following the next sitting. Lynam refers to herself as a 'fully qualified CFA who holds the Charter'. Who has breached CFA Institute Code and Standards?

   A. Parrot only.

   B. Lynam only.

   C. Lynam and Parrot.

10. Anderb Costello, a portfolio manager for XYZ Investment Management Company – a registered investment organization that advises investment companies and private accounts – was promoted to that position three years ago. Joanna Bates, her supervisor, is responsible for reviewing Costello's portfolio account transactions, and her required monthly reports of personal stock transactions. Costello has been using Jonelli Patel, a broker, almost exclusively for portfolio account brokerage transactions. For securities in which Patel's firm makes a market, Patel has been giving Costello lower prices for personal purchases and higher prices for personal sales than Patel gives Costello's portfolio accounts and other investors. Costello has been filing monthly reports with Bates only in those months in which she has no personal transactions, which is about every fourth month. Which one of the following statements is *least accurate*?

   A. Patel violated the Code and Standards providing Costello with favorable transaction prices.

   B. Costello violated the Code and Standards in that she failed to disclose to her employer her personal transactions.

   C. Costello violated the Code and Standards by breaching her fiduciary duty to her clients.

11. Which one of the following statements about the use of soft dollars is *least accurate*?

   A. The client may direct the investment manager to use the client's brokerage to purchase goods/services for the client.

   B. Brokerage commissions may be directed to pay for the investment manager's operating expenses.

   C. Brokerage commissions may be directed to pay for securities research used in managing the client's portfolio.

12. John Vickery, a trustee for the pension plan of Richardson Industries, has just received a commission schedule from XYZ Brokerage, a firm with which he is not now trading. The fee schedule is lower than the schedule of ABC Brokerage, which is the firm Vickery now uses for most transactions. ABC also provides research data and performance measurement for the pension plan, services that XYZ cannot handle. Vickery is concerned that he may be violating his fiduciary duty of loyalty by not using the lowest cost brokerage firm. Based on the Standards of Professional Conduct, which of the following statements is *most accurate*?

   A. Vickery will violate his fiduciary duty unless he immediately begins trading through XYZ.

   B. Vickery will not violate his fiduciary duty unless he personally profits from his relationship with ABC.

   C. Vickery can continue to trade through ABC if he determines, in good faith, that the value of the services is commensurate with the cost.

13. Bob Ryan CFA, is an analyst with a large insurance company. His personal portfolio includes a significant investment in the common stock of QRS Company, which his firm does not now follow. The director of the insurance company's research department asks Ryan to analyze QRS and write a report about its investment potential. Based on the Standards of Professional Conduct, Ryan should:

   A. Place his shares of QRS in a trust.

   B. Sell his shares of QRS before completing the report.

   C. Disclose the ownership of the stock to his employer and in the report.

14. Which of the following is the *most accurate* definition of information in the context of material nonpublic information?

A. Disclosure of the information would be likely to have an impact on the price of the security or reasonable investors would want to know the information prior to making an investment decision.

B. Information which would cause the price of the security to move by in excess of 10%.

C. Information which is derived from confidential discussions between the receiver of the Information and the issuer.

15. Which of the following is *most accurate* with respect to Standard I.A – Knowledge of the Law?

It requires:

I   Members should have an understanding of the laws and regulations of countries in which they operate.

II Members should report legal violations to appropriate regulatory organizations.

	STATEMENT I	STATEMENT II
A.	True	False
B.	True	True
C.	False	True

16. Duncan Yates is a passionate private pilot who spends all his free time flying or helping to run his local flying club. Because of his interest, his employer, Emport Fund Management, has given him the role of analyzing aviation stocks. He has just completed a positive report on New Fly Inc, a company that is hoping to revolutionize recreational flying by developing cheap, self-build aircraft kits. New Fly Inc is based at Yate's local airfield and he has always, as a keen flyer, taken an interest in their work and has even helped them in certain development matters. To a large extent, his positive outlook is based on a belief and hope that the company will succeed. On the evidence based above, which of the following Standards is Yates *most likely* to have breached?

A. Standard V.B – Communication with Clients and Prospective Clients as he has failed to distinguish between fact and opinion in his report.

B. Standard V.C – Record Retention as he has failed to properly develop and maintain appropriate records to support his analysis.

C. Standard V.A – Diligence and Reasonable Basis as he has failed to thoroughly analyze the investment.

17. Which one of the following statements is *most accurate* in respect of Standard III.B – Fair Dealing?

A. If different service levels are offered to clients, disclosure of the service levels must be disclosed but do not need to be offered to all clients.

B. It is appropriate to allocate some shares in an over subscribed new issue to family members as long as none are allocated to the Member themselves.

C. Members can offer more personal and specialized service to clients willing to pay a premium service through higher levels of fees.

18. Which of the following is *most likely* to be a standard of competence which a CFA Institute member should reach in order to satisfy his or her ethical responsibilities under Standard 1A – Knowledge of the Law?

    A. Becoming an expert in compliance.

    B. Having detailed knowledge of all laws that could potentially govern the member's conduct.

    C. Having an understanding of applicable laws and regulations in all countries where the member provides investment services.

19. Dana Simpson leaves her employment at Boco Bank, where she has developed an analytical model allowing her to detect undervalued stocks in the emerging market, to join a rival bank. Which of the following statements is *most accurate*?

    A. Simpson cannot under any circumstances use the model she developed whilst at Boco.

    B. If Simpson recreates her work and all the supporting records of her original model she can use it at her new employer.

    C. Simpson can use the model but only if she publicly acknowledges that it is Boco Bank's model and not a model developed by her current employer.

20. John Williams CFA uses a very complicated system to appraise securities, yet does not explain it properly in the research report. Which Standard is John *most likely* to have breached?

    A. Standard III.B – Fair Dealing.

    B. Standard V.B – Communication with Clients and Prospective Clients.

    C. Standard V.A – Diligence and Reasonable Basis.

21. Yellow Securities has the following three policies, which one of the following is *most likely* to be in conflict with CFA Institute standards?

    A. Analysts may change their investment recommendations without obtaining approval from their supervisor.

    B. Personal account transactions by analysts should not be scrutinized for confidentiality reasons.

    C. A portfolio manager should conduct a fact-find about a new customer before undertaking investment action on the customer's behalf.

22. Which of the following is *least likely* to assist fair treatment of clients when a material change to a previous investment recommendation is being made?

    A. Shortening the time frame between the decision to make the recommendation and disseminating the recommendation.

    B. Monitoring the trading activities of firm personnel.

    C. Appointing one person at the firm to make material changes to recommendations.

23. Rachel Goldman CFA is meeting a new client for the first time. Having noted down details of the client's name, address, telephone number, and salary, Goldman tells the client that she has identified a good new investment which she is recommending to the client. Goldman could have avoided a violation of Standards implied by these actions by:

    A. Determining the client's needs, objectives and key investment requirements prior to making the recommendation.

    B. Identifying if any previous investment adviser had caused Goldman's investment portfolio to perform badly, possibly through breaching CFA Institute Standards.

    C. Explaining the detailed liquidity, dividend, income and risk characteristics of the investment prior to making the recommendation.

24. Which one of following statements is *least likely* to breach a member's duty to an employer?

    A. Initiating an employee-led buyout of an employing firm while still employed by the firm.

    B. Soliciting potential clients for a new firm while still employed by an existing employer.

    C. Approaching other employees to initiate an employee walkout.

25. You have noticed that your client is breaking the law. However, the local law states the client confidentiality is required in all circumstances. You believe that the Code and Standards require you to break your duty of confidentiality when a law has been broken. You further believe that a breach of confidentiality is permissible when it is in the client's benefit. Which of the following statements is *most appropriate*?

    A. Both of your beliefs are incorrect.

    B. Only your first belief about breaching confidentiality when a law has been broken is correct.

    C. Only your second belief about breaching a confidentiality when it is in the client's best interest is correct.

26. Kevin Doyle CFA is an investment manager providing discretionary management services for his clients. One of his clients gives him an expensive bottle of whiskey as a present after exceptional performance for his portfolio. Doyle accepts the present but does not disclose the present to his employer.

    Doyle has *most likely*:

    A. Not breached Standard 1B – Independence and Objectivity.

    B. Breached Standard 1B – Independence and Objectivity by accepting the present.

    C. Breached Standard 1B – Independence and Objectivity by not disclosing the present to his employer.

27. Based on Standard III.E – Preservation of Confidentiality, an analyst must preserve the confidentiality of information received from clients when two criteria are met. First, the analyst and client must be in a relationship of trust and second, the:

    A. Information received by the analyst must result from, or be relevant to, the portion of the client's business that relates to the special or confidential relationship.

    B. Full disclosure would indicate that the best interest of customers, clients, and employers have been served rather than that of the analyst.

    C. Information could impair the analyst's ability to render unbiased and objected advice.

28. Standard VI.B – Priority of Transactions covers activities of all members who have knowledge of pending transactions or 'access' to information. Which one of the following would be considered an 'access' person?

    A. An independent auditor that has access to material nonpublic information.

    B. A supervisor of analysts that reviews all research reports prior to dissemination.

    C. An analyst who has a beneficial ownership of securities in a company that she covers.

29. James Harper CFA has told his client Frank Van Vleit that his investments in US Treasury Bonds are guaranteed to be repaid on their final maturity as they are backed by the full faith and credit of the US government. Harper has told his client Don Zappa that he guarantees that his equity portfolio will not show a negative return over a time period of 30 years or more.

    Harper has breached Standard IC – Misrepresentation in respect of his statement to:

	VAN VLIET	ZAPPA
A.	Yes	Yes
B.	No	No
C.	No	Yes

30. James Bryon CFA is an investment manager providing discretionary management services for clients. There is a hot new equity initial public offering (IPO) for which he has received an allocation of shares. The issue is oversubscribed and so it is not possible for all of Bryon's clients to receive their full allocation. As a result, Bryon allocates shares pro rata to his clients and his own personal account to ensure that no one is disadvantaged.

    Bryon has

    A. Not violated Standard IIIB – Fair Dealing.

    B. Violated Standard IIIB – Fair Dealing by allocating a pro rata share of the allocation to his own personal account.

    C. Violated Standard IIIB – Fair Dealing by allocating a pro rata share of the allocation to both his clients and to his own personal account.

31. A firm has been in existence for eight years. It started preparing performance presentation standards in compliance with GIPS last year. What is the minimum number of years of performance history it should show in this year's performance presentation?

    A. Five years.

    B. Six years.

    C. Eight years.

32. When local regulations require a presentation that is in conflict with a GIPS requirement, a firm wishing to claim compliance with GIPS should:

    A. Follows the requirements of GIPS.

    B. Follow the local requirements.

    C. Follow the local requirements and disclose the impact of this.

Quantitative Analysis

33. The rate of interest for a repayment mortgage of $100,000 over 20 years is 7%. Which of the following is *closest to* the annual repayment required at the end of each year?

   A. $2,439

   B. $9,439

   C. $12,000

34. Which of the following answers is *closest to* the coefficient of variation of the following population?

   5, 7, 13, 29, 40

   A. 0.10

   B. 0.72

   C. 13.54

35. If the stated rate is 9% and the compounding interval is monthly, which of the following is *closest to* the effective annual rate?

   A. 9.0%

   B. 9.3%

   C. 9.4%

36. A project involves an initial outlay of $10,000 and the following inflows at the end of each year, starting in one year's time: $3,000, $4,000, $5,000, $6,000. Which of the following *is closest to* the project's IRR?

   A. 18.3%

   B. 22.7%

   C. 24.9%

37. A flow of $2,000 in two years' time has a net present value of $1,624. Assuming continuous compounding, which of the following is *closest to* the annual percentage rate?

   A. 10.4%

   B. 10.7%

   C. 10.9%

38. The present value of an annuity due lasting ten years with an interest rate of 5% is $8,108. Which of the following is *closest to* the present value of an ordinary annuity with the same cash flow lasting the same number of years and with the same interest rate?

   A. $7,720

   B. $8,110

   C. $8,510

39. An individual deposits $1,500 today and $1,500 one year from today into an interest-earning account. The deposits earn 12 percent compounded annually. If $500 is then withdrawn each year beginning two years from today, the balance in the account ten years from today is *closest to*:

    A. −$1,500

    B. $544

    C. $1,431

40. The following sample data relate to the sales and profit of a small manufacturing company.

	JAN	FEB	MAR	APR
Sales (in thousands of dollars)	1,000	1,300	1,700	2,000
Profit (in thousands of dollars)	165	215	270	350

    The sample covariance of sales and profit is *closest to*

    A. 25,875

    B. 34,500

    C. 88,125

41. Given a data series that is normally distributed with a mean of 100 and a standard deviation of 10, about 95% of the numbers in the series will fall within:

    A. 60 to 140

    B. 70 to 130

    C. 80 to 120

42. A portfolio had a beginning market value of $400,000, after the client has withdrawn $100,000 from the portfolio. At the end of the first year, the portfolio paid out a dividend of $20,000 and had a market value after this of $390,000. At the end of the second year, the market value of the portfolio is $430,000, before a dividend is paid out of $30,000. Which of the following is *closest to* the time weighted rate of return for the portfolio?

    A. 6.2%

    B. 6.3%

    C. 13.0%

43. Which one of the following statements is *most accurate*?

    A. Both the mode and the mean are distorted by extreme values.

    B. Both the mode and the mean will be greater then the median for a positively skewed population.

    C. Both the mode and the mean provide an indication of central tendency.

44. The probability of a Type I error is 5%. The probability of a Type II error is 20%. What is the power of the test?

    A. 20%.

    B. 80%.

    C. 95%.

45. A distribution has a mean of 120 and a variance of 100. Which of the following is *closest to* the range of values within which at least 75% of observations will lie?

   A. 113 to 127

   B. 100 to 140

   C. 20 to 220

46. Which of the following is a sentiment indicator?

   A. Stochastic oscillator.

   B. Bollinger bands.

   C. Put/call ratio.

47. Which of the following statements is/are *most accurate*?

   I   Collective exhaustibility states that all probabilities together sum to one

   II   If working out the probability of rolling a six on a dice, a priori probabilities would be more appropriate than empirical probabilities.

	STATEMENT I	STATEMENT II
A.	True	False
B.	False	True
C.	True	True

48. Which of the following statements regarding the sample size is *least accurate*?

   A. A larger sample size will reduce the test statistic.

   B. A larger sample size will make it easier to reject the null hypothesis.

   C. A larger sample size is likely to give more reliable results.

49. The probability of a student passing a test is 70%. If eight students take the test, and the success of each student is independent of the other students, what is the probability that more than six of them will pass?

   A. 0.082

   B. 0.013

   C. 0.256

50. Which of the following measurement scales enable data to be categorized and ranked, but for which the intervals between values are not equal?

   A. Ordinal scales.

   B. Interval scales.

   C. Nominal scales.

BPP
LEARNING MEDIA

51. Which of the following is *closest to* the harmonic mean of the following values? 2, 4, 5, 7.
    A. 3.7.
    B. 4.1.
    C. 4.5.

52. A hypothesis test has rejected a null hypothesis at the 1% level (one-tailed test). Which of the following is correct in respect of the hypothesized mean μ?
    A. The hypothesized mean is 1.96 SE away from the sample mean.
    B. The hypothesized mean is 2.33 SE away from the sample mean.
    C. The hypothesized mean is 2.58 SE away from the sample mean.

53. Where a distribution has excess kurtosis of −1, the distribution is:
    A. Mesokurtic.
    B. Platykurtic.
    C. Leptokurtic.

54. There is a probability of 0.2 that a company's credit rating will increase from AA to AAA in the first year. If the company's credit rating does increase in the first year, there is a 0.6 probability that it will remain AAA in the second year. If it does not increase in the first year, there is a 0.2 probability it will increase to AAA in the second year. Which of the following is *closest to* the probability that the company's credit rating will be below AAA in the second year?
    A. 0.08
    B. 0.72
    C. 0.80

55. Which of the following statements is *most accurate*. The lognormal distribution:
    A. Is symmetrical.
    B. Has a right skew.
    C. Has a left skew.

56. In which of the following circumstances is the assumption that the sampling distribution of sample means is normally distributed likely to be most appropriate? The variance of the:
    A. Population is unknown and the sample size is large.
    B. Normally distributed population is known and the sample size is small.
    C. Normally distributed population is unknown and the sample size is large.

57. Which of the following is the *most complete and accurate* definition of a hypothesis in relation to statistical testing? A hypothesis is a statement about a population that:
    A. Cannot be disproved.
    B. Can be proved to a specified error level.
    C. Can be disproved at a specified error level.

Equity

58. When the rate of return is above the equilibrium rate, it is *most likely* that there will be:

    A. More savers than borrowers and the interest rate will fall.

    B. More savers than borrowers and the interest rate will rise.

    C. More borrowers than savers and the interest rate will rise.

59. Preferred stock *most likely*:

    A. Have voting rights.

    B. Receive a fixed dividend.

    C. Have a residual interest in the assets of the issuer.

60. The initial margin is 20%. A stock increases in price by 50%. The profit to the margined transaction is *closest to*:

    A. 100%.

    B 200%.

    C. 250%.

61. Which of the following index weighting methods has the disadvantage that securities whose price has risen the most have a greater weight in the index?

    A Fundamental weighting.

    B. Market capitalization weighting.

    C. Equal weighting.

62. Details of a limit order book are as follows.

BIDS		OFFERS	
QUANTITY	PRICE	PRICE	QUANTITY
100	52	54	540
250	51	56	100
120	49	57	100

An investor submits a limit sell order for 400 shares at a price of 50. The total price paid for the shares purchased is *closest to:*

    A $17,500.

    B. $17,950.

    C. $20,000.

63. Which of the following *best describes* a market where trades can occur at any time?

    A. Call market.

    B. Auction market.

    C. Continuous market.

64. Rebalancing is *most likely* a major issue for an index that is:
    A. Price weighted.
    B. Equal weighted.
    C. Market capitalization weighted.

65. Market efficiency is *most likely* higher when:
    A. Trading costs are high.
    B. Short stock positions are permitted.
    C. Arbitrage activity is not commonly undertaken.

66. Which of the following levels of market efficiency would *most likely* imply that it may be possible to make supernormal profits by investing in low price to book stocks?
    A. Weak form only.
    B. Weak form and semi-strong form only.
    C. Weak form, semi-strong form and strong form.

67. The January anomaly *most likely* suggests that:
    A. Stocks will earn lower than average returns in January.
    B. Investors sell stocks for tax reasons during the month of January.
    C. Investors should buy stocks in December and sell them in January.

68. Compared to real returns on government bonds, real returns on equities over time have *most likely* been:
    A. Higher and more volatile.
    B. Higher but not more volatile.
    C. Approximately the same but more volatile.

69. Different classes of common stock in a company:
    A. May have different dividend rights and different voting rights.
    B. Will have the same dividend rights and the same voting rights.
    C. Will have the same dividend rights but must have different voting rights.

70. Which of the following is *least similar* to common stock?
    A. Convertible preference shares.
    B. Cumulative preference shares.
    C. Participating preference shares.

71. Level I sponsored ADRs *most likely*:
    A. Only trade in the over the counter (OTC) market.
    B. Are subject to full registration requirements with the SEC.
    C. Are subject to size requirements before being eligible for trading.

72. Issuing common equity will *most likely* increase a company's:

    A. Book value.

    B. Common stock price.

    C. Book value and common stock price.

73. Statistical techniques for placing companies into industry groups are designed such that companies in the same group have:

    A. Low correlations with each other and different groups have low correlations with each other.

    B. High correlations with each other and different groups have low correlations with each other.

    C. High correlations with each other and different groups have high correlations with each other.

74. Return on invested capital is *most likely* to be high in an industry where barriers to exit are:

    A. Low and customer bargaining power is low.

    B Low and customer bargaining power is high.

    C. High and customer bargaining power is high.

75. An analyst expects a company to pay a dividend per share next year of $2.00. The dividend in two years time is expected to be $2.10 and the dividend in three years time is expected to be $2.30. The stock price is expected to be $27.00 in three years time. The required return on the stock is 9%. The estimate of intrinsic value for the stock is *closest to*:

    A. $24.51.

    B. $26.23.

    C. $26.71.

76. A company has a high level of intangible assets but is not currently paying a dividend. The valuation method that is *most likely* to be appropriate is the:

    A. Asset based approach.

    B. Present value approach using dividends.

    C. Present value approach using free cash flow.

77. A company is paying dividends that will be constant for two years, then grow at a constant rate indefinitely. An investment horizon of two years will give an intrinsic value for the stock compared to an investment horizon of 10 years will *most likely* be:

    A Lower.

    B. Higher.

    C. The same.

78. A company has just paid a common stock dividend of $10.00 per share. The dividend is expected to grow at a rate of 2% and the required rate of return on the common stock is 7%. The intrinsic value of the common stock is *closest to*:

    A $146.

    B. $200.

    C. $204.

Financial Statement Analysis

79. A company has a current ratio of 1.7. Which of the following is *most likely* to cause the current ratio to increase?

   A. Paying off accounts payable from the cash balance.

   B. Collecting cash from accounts receivable.

   C. Selling inventories on credit.

80. During a period of rising prices and stable inventory levels, a company using FIFO accounting compared to a company using LIFO accounting is *most likely* to show:

   A. Higher inventory values and higher gross profit.

   B. Higher inventory values and lower gross profit.

   C. Lower inventory values and lower gross profit.

81. Capitalization of interest in a year compared to non-capitalization will cause a firm to have:

   A. Higher assets and lower equity.

   B. Higher assets and higher equity.

   C. Lower assets and lower equity.

82. Which of the following is *least likely* to be true with respect to a finance lease?

   A. An asset will be recognised on the balance sheet of the lessee.

   B. Payments under the leasse are split into an interest and capital element, the interest element being charged against income and the capital element being treated as a repayment of debt.

   C. Payments under the lease are shown as financing cash flows in the cash flow statement.

83. Which one of the following statements is *least accurate* with respect to straight-line depreciation adopted by companies?

   A. It gives a rising return on equity over the life of the asset.

   B. It assumes an equal benefit is being received in each year of the asset's life.

   C. It will cause cash flows over the life of the asset to remain constant.

84. The following information has been extracted from the financial statements of Lazydog Inc.

	$
Long-lived asset cost	100,000
Accumulated depreciation	35,000

   Assuming that Lazydog Inc applies straight-line depreciation and that the remaining life of assets is 13 years, which of the following statements is *closest* to the depreciation charge for the year?

   A. $0

   B. $5,000

   C. $40,000

The following information is required to answer Questions 85 and 86.

	$
Accounts receivable at 31.12 Year 2	300
Accounts payable at 31.12 Year 2	600
Inventories at 31.12 Year 2	100
Interest paid/payable	2,000
Earnings before interest and tax	10,000
Dividends paid	200
Capital expenditure	1,000
Depreciation expense	1,000
Net book value of fixed assets sold	500
Share issues during the year	3,000
Loans repaid during the year	700
Accounts receivable at 31.12 Year 1	280
Accounts payable at 31.12 Year 1	550
Inventories at 31.12 Year 1	200

The tax rate is 30% of income before tax. Included in earnings is a loss on disposal of fixed assets of $50. The company follows US GAAP accounting.

85. What is cash flow from operations?

    A. $6,680

    B. $6,730

    C. $6,780

86. What are the financing cash flows?

    A. $2,100

    B. $2,300

    C. $2,800

87. Compared to using an operating lease, a lesee that uses finance leases will *most likely* report higher:

    A. Current liabilities.

    B. Current assets.

    C. Cost of sales.

88. If companies use straight-line depreciation instead of double declining balance in times of rising prices, which of the following is *most likely* to be higher?

    A. Cash flows from operations.

    B. Total asset turnover.

    C. Retained earnings.

89. Which of the following is *most accurate* when inventory prices are rising?

    A. FIFO firms will report lower cost of sales than LIFO firms.

    B. FIFO firms will report lower inventory ending than LIFO firms.

    C. LIFO firms will report higher gross profit than FIFO firms.

90. If a company issues a zero-coupon bond rather than a coupon bond, which of the following statements is *most accurate*?

    A. There will be no difference in the cash flow since it is the yield to maturity of the bond that impacts the cash flow.

    B. The company's operating cash flow will be understated.

    C. The company's operating cash flow will be overstated.

91. An asset is to be leased under a finance lease. The life of the asset is ten years and the lease is for nine years. At the end of the lease the asset reverts to the lessor. The fair value of the asset is $90,000 and the present value of the minimum lease payments is $80,000. Which of the following is closest to the depreciation expense in the income statement of the leasee each year (assuming straight line depreciation)?

    A. $8,000

    B. $8,888

    C. $9,000

92. Net margin is 5%. Total asset turnover is 3×. Return on equity is 22.5%. Which of the following is *closest to* the financial leverage?

    A. 0.1×

    B. 0.7×

    C. 1.5×

93. A company's return on equity increases in the year. Taking each in isolation, which of the following is *least likely* to have contributed to this increase?

    A. The tax burden changing from 0.7 to 0.65.

    B. An increase in return on assets.

    C. An increase in total assets.

94. Which of the following is *least likely* to be disclosed separately within the statement of changes in owners' equity?

    A. Unrealised gain on investments.

    B. Minority interest.

    C. Realised exchange gains on overseas purchases.

95. Which of the following is *least likely* to be included in an analyst's review of a technology company that has significant stock options?

    A. Size of cash inflow included within the operating cash flow statement that relates to the tax benefit on options exercised in the period.

    B. Review of deferred tax provision for impact of options outstanding.

    C. Review of notes to establish volume of options exercised during the period.

96. The following details relate to a company's property, plant and equipment.

    Net book value at December 31 2011 $1,000

    Net book value at December 31 2012 $1,200

    During 2012, the company bought assets costing $500 and sold assets, receiving proceeds of $50 and making a profit on disposal of $30. What was the depreciation expense in 2012?

    A. $200

    B. $220

    C. $280

97. Which of the following is the *most likely* to decrease when there is a rise in the valuation allowance related to a deferred tax asset, all else being equal?

    A. Total asset turnover.

    B. Cash flow from operations.

    C. Net income.

98. Which of the following is *least likely* to be a warning sign of accounting irregularities?

    A. Cash flow earnings index (operating cash flow/net income) is consistently above 1.

    B. Steady increase in inventory levels when sales revenue is in decline.

    C. Recording revenue when sales contract is signed and goods are yet to be despatched.

99. MSG Inc had 4.25m common stock in issue on January 1 2011. On April 1 2011, it issued a further 1.25m common stock at full price. On May 1 2011, MSG Inc completed a 5 for 3 stock split. The financial statements, published in July 2012, showed net income for the year ended December 31 2011 of $1.31m. MSG Inc has no preferred stock in issue. The common stock dividend for 2011 was $0.75m. MSG Inc EPS for 2011 is *closest to*:

    A. $0.15.

    B. $0.20.

    C. $0.22.

100. Which of the following statements about deferred taxes is *most accurate*?

Deferred taxes:

A. Are required by the IRS.

B. Facilitate calculation of income tax expense.

C. Are provided for both temporary and permanent timing differences.

101. Which of the following would *least likely* require a retrospective adjustment to accounts?

A. A change in the estimated useful life of a fixed asset.

B. A change from an incorrect accounting method to a correct one.

C. A change in the method of inventory allocation.

102. Which of the following is *most accurate* of goodwill?

A. The amortization period should not exceed 20 years.

B. Internally developed goodwill can be capitalized.

C. It reduces net income in the period in which it becomes impaired.

103. Under US GAAP, what is the best definition of impairment in respect of long-lived assets?

A. Where the future discounted cash flows generated from the asset exceed the carrying amount on the balance sheet.

B. Where the future cash flows generated from the assets are below the carrying amount on the balance sheet.

C. Where the recoverable amount from an asset falls below the future undiscounted cash flows generated from the asset.

104. Which of the following is *most likely* to be classified as liquidity ratio?

A. Interest coverage.

B. Financial leverage ratio.

C. Quick ratio.

105. What will be the deferred tax asset reported in the accounts if a company has total taxable losses carried forward of $60,000, $35,000 of which are more likely than not to be realized and the tax rate is 30%?

A. $7,500

B. $10,500

C. $18,500

106. Three start-up companies in the same industry and using the same new assets adopt three different depreciation methods for their first year of accounts:

COMPANY	DEPRECIATION METHOD
X	Double-declining
Y	Straight-line
Z	Units of production (with low levels of production in the early years)

Assuming that all three companies achieve the same level of sales and have the same operating expenses other than depreciation, which company is *most likely* to have the highest asset turnover and *lowest* profit margin in Year 1 of operation?

A. X

B. Y

C. Z

107. When a deferred tax liability falls, which of the following effects is *most likely*?

A. Tax paid in the cash flow statement and tax charged in the income statement will be the same.

B. The tax rate has just been increased.

C. Taxes payable will exceed tax expense.

108. On December 31, a company charges through its income statement $5m for the write-down of assets. Which of the following statements is *most accurate*?

A. Income in prior years is likely to have been overstated.

B. Income is likely to be understated while income in prior years is likely to have been overstated.

C. Income is likely to be overstated while income in prior years is likely to have been understated.

109. A company's return on equity is currently 2%. The company now takes on two long-term contracts for which there are contracts of sale. Contract A is expected to be one of the most profitable that the company has undertaken but it turns out that Contract B is expected to breakeven in its earlier years but to make losses in its later years. Which of the following is the *most likely* impact of the contracts on return on equity in the short term?

A. Contract A will increase ROE.

B. Contract B will increase ROE.

C. The impact of both contracts on ROE cannot be determined.

110. Which of the following is *most likely* to boost a company's cash flow from operations?

A. Regular securitising of receivables.

B. Regular stock buy backs to offset the dilution effect of share options being exercised.

C. Reduction in the average credit period taken from suppliers.

111. A lessee entering a finance lease as opposed to an operating lease will have:

A. lower cash flow from operations.

B. a larger asset base.

C. lower cash flow from investing activities.

112. An analyst wishes to establish a growth screen for a global equity index. Which of the following criterion is *least likely* to be used in the screen?

   A. Consensus forecast EPS growth % > 8%.

   B. Current P/E < median P/E of all stocks in the index.

   C. Current ROE % > median ROE of all stocks in the index.

113. Which of the following is *most likely* to occur when an analyst makes an adjustment to a company's set of accounts to treat inventory on a FIFO basis rather than on a LIFO basis? The company has faced continual rising inventory prices over its history and inventory levels have been constant.

   A. Current ratio will decrease.

   B. Cost of sales will increase.

   C. Year-end inventory value will increase.

114. Which of the following statements is *least accurate* regarding the accruals method of accounting?

   A. Income reported is a more realistic picture of the firm's current operating results.

   B. Revenue is recorded when it is generated; expenses are recorded when they are incurred.

   C. Cash flows can be allocated to periods other than those in which they occur.

115. Which one of the following is *least likely* to be capitalised rather than expensed?

   A. Delivery cost of a machine

   B. Testing cost of a machine

   C. Staff training of a machine

116. Which of the following statements regarding common size statements is *least accurate*?

   A. They are not required to be presented in the face of the financial statements by IAS GAAP.

   B. They ease comparison of changes in component accounts from one period to the next.

   C. They ease calculation of financial ratios, such as total asset turnover and return on common equity.

117. Which of the following is *least accurate* with respect to the percentage of completion method as compared to the completed contract method?

   A. It will give higher stockholder's equity over the life of the contract.

   B. It will give higher assets over the life of the contract.

   C. It must be used for all long-term contracts.

118. If an analyst adjusts a set of accounts to bring operating leases onto the balance sheet, which of the following is *most likely* to be observed?

   A. Total asset turnover will increase.

   B. Interest coverage will decrease.

   C. Operating leverage will increase.

119. Which of the following would be classified as a current liability?

    A. Unearned revenue.

    B. Prepaid expenses.

    C. Accrued revenue.

120. When a company recognizes income more quickly than is appropriate under the accruals concept, which one of the following is *most accurate*?

    A. Cash from operations will be overstated.

    B. Shareholders' equity will be understated.

    C. Receivables will be overstated.

Ethical and Professional Standards

1. **A**   Standard III.E Preservation of Confidentiality. Note that the standard does not prevent members from cooperating with the CFA Institute's Professional Conduct Program.

    LOS 2a

2. **B**   GIPS, like the Code and Standards, is based on self-regulation, rather than regulation enforced by CFA Institute.

    LOS 4a

3. **A**   Standard III.E Preservation of Confidentiality.

    LOS 2a

4. **C**   Standard II.A Material Nonpublic Information. Ensure you know the definition of mosaic theory as it is regularly tested.

    LOS 2a

5. **B**   Standard IV.C Responsibilities of Supervisors. The standard states that although members and candidates may delegate duties they are not relieved of supervisory responsibility.

    LOS 2a

6. **B**   All proxies should be voted in an informed and responsible manner. It may be appropriate to do a cost-benefit analysis on whether voting on all proxies is in the clients' best interests, but this statement on proxies does not appear well considered. Regarding soft dollar practices, these are acceptable as long as disclosed. It would be a violation if the member/candidate pays more for the services without the corresponding benefit to the client.

    LOS 2a

7. **C**   Standard VI.A Disclosure of Conflicts. Lisa should inform her clients of the changes in her compensation arrangements with her employer that have created a conflict of interest.

    LOS 2a

8. **C**   Standard I.B Independence and Objectivity. The best option is to avoid any risk of a perceived lack of objectivity. The standard specifically refers to analyst using commercial transport rather than accepting paid travel arrangements.

    LOS 2a

9. **C**   Standard VII.B Responsibilities as a CFA Institute member or CFA candidate. John is not a CFA candidate. Janet has referred to herself as a 'CFA'.

    LOS 2a

10. **A**   By not disclosing personal transactions as required, Anderb has breached Standard I.D – Misconduct. She has also breached Standard III.A – Loyalty, Prudence and Care with her personal transactions and Bates has breached Standard IV.C – Responsibilities of Supervisors.

    LOS 2a

11. **B** Standard III.A – Loyalty, Prudence and Care. Soft dollars are generally allowed for acquiring research for the benefit of clients.

LOS 2a

12. **C** Standard III.A – Loyalty, Prudence and Care. The primary responsibilities of John Vickery are a duty of loyalty and a duty to exercise reasonable care. As long as he determines that the value of the services from ABC is commensurate with the costs, he can continue to use ABC.

LOS 2a

13. **C** Standard VI.A – Disclosure of Conflicts. The standard states that prohibiting members/candidates from owning securities is overly prohibitive, but that they should disclose any material beneficial holdings in securities they recommend. This holding is clearly material.

LOS 2a

14. **A** Standard II.A – Material nonpublic information.

LOS 2a

15. **A** Standard I.A says members should dissociate from any illegal activity. There is no requirement to report legal violations to the relevant authorities.

LOS 2a

16. **C** Standard V.A – Diligence and Reasonable Basis. From the evidence, the only Standard that Duncan has breached is Standard V.A. If, as suggested, he has based his report on his interest and involvement then this would suggest a lack of diligence and thorough analysis. The question mentions nothing about the content or the records that he has kept.

LOS 2a

17. **C** Standard III.B – Fair Dealing. Service levels cannot be offered selectively, but there is nothing wrong with having different service levels as it is disclosed to all clients.

LOS 2a

18. **C** Standard IA – Knowledge of the Law. Members are not expected to become experts in compliance or have a detailed knowledge of all laws that might potentially govern their conduct.

LOS 1c

19. **B** Standard IV.A Loyalty. If Dana recreates the model and all the appropriate records then she may use it.

LOS 2a

20. **B** If a complex system is used, its key features should be highlighted to enable clients to understand what has been done.

LOS 2a

21. **B** Standard IV.C – Responsibilities of Supervisors. Checks should be carried out by supervisors.

LOS 2a

22. **C** Standard III.B – Fair Dealing. There is no requirement to appoint a single person to be responsible for material changes, but the other two options are specifically referred to in the recommended procedures for compliance.

LOS 2a

23. **A** Standard III.C – Suitability. Clearly Goldman has not undertaken a thorough analysis of the client's needs and objectives.

LOS 2a

24. **A** Standard IV.A – Loyalty. Note that a buy-out concerns a change in ownership, which is not undermining the employer. A walk-out is more disruptive to the employer's operations.

LOS 2a

25. **A** Standard III.E – Preservation of Confidentiality. The Standard does not require Members to break the duty of confidentiality when a law has been broken.

LOS 2a

26. **C** Standard IB – Independence and Objectivity. Members can accept gifts from clients but must disclose these to their employers.

LOS 1,c and LOS 2a,b,c

27. **A** Standard III.E – Preservation of Confidentiality applies when the member receives information on the basis of his or her special ability to conduct a portion of the client's business or personal affairs and the member receives information that arises from, or is relevant to, that portion of the client's business that is the subject of the special or confidential relationship. If the information concerns illegal activities by the client, however, the member may have an obligation to report the activities to the appropriate authorities. The most conservative and effective way to comply with Standard III.E is to avoid disclosing any information received from a client, except to authorized fellow employees who are also working with the client.

LOS 2a

28. **B** An individual is considered to be an 'access' or 'covered' person if they have knowledge of pending or actual investment recommendations or action. An auditor may have inside information, but that is not relevant to this scenario about investment recommendations.

LOS 2a

29. **C** Standard IC – Misrepresentation. It is permitted to make statements about guarantees that are built into a product. However, it is a misrepresentation to make guarantees about returns on products that are inherently unstable.

LOS 2a,b

30. **B** Standard IIIB – Fair Dealing. When there is an oversubscribed issue, the member should forgo his own allocation to free up shares for clients.

LOS 2a,b

31. **B** GIPS. Five years in the first year plus one additional year.

LOS 4a,b

32.   **C**   GIPS. A firm wishing to claim compliance with GIPS should follow the local requirements and disclose the impact of this.

   LOS 4c

Quantitative Analysis

33. **B**   N = 20,   1000 = PV,   7 =I/Y,   CPT PMT = −9,439

See LOS 5f

34. **B**

X	$(x-\bar{x})$	$(x-\bar{x})^2$
5	−13.8	190.44
7	−11.8	139.24
13	−5.8	33.64
29	10.2	104.04
40	21.2	449.44
94		916.80

$$\bar{X} = \frac{94}{5} = 18.8 \qquad \sigma = \Sigma\frac{\sigma(x-\bar{x})^2}{n} = \sqrt{\frac{916.8}{5}} = 13.54$$

Coefficient of variation = $\dfrac{\sigma}{\bar{X}}$ = $\dfrac{13.54}{18.8}$ = 0.72

See LOS 7i

35. **C** $\left(1+\dfrac{0.09}{12}\right)^{12} - 1 = 0.0938$. The monthly rate ($r_m$) is given by 9% ÷ 12. The effective annual rate is calculated as $(1 + r_m)^{12} - 1$.

LOS 5c

36. **C**   Use your calculator to obtain the IRR based on the cash flows

TIME	FLOW
0	(10,000)
1	3,000
2	4,000
3	5,000
4	6,000

LOS 6a

37. **A**   Try each answer in turn: $1624e^{(0.104 \times 2)} = 2000$ or solve $2r = LN(2000/1624)$

LOS 5c

38. **A**   An ordinary annuity has its cash flows one year later than an annuity due. Therefore, each cash flow has to be discounted back by one more year compared to the annuity due. Therefore the present value of the ordinary annuity will be: $\dfrac{8,108}{1.05} = 7,722$. A longer way of calculating this would be to calculate the annual cash flow for the annuity due and then to re-work the present value calculation for the ordinary annuity.

LOS 5e

39.   C   Using the CF function:

CF0 = 1500

C01 = 1500   F01 = 1

C02 = -500   F02 = 9

Use the NFV calculation (as per NPV calculation but one down arrow from NPV after entering the interest rate).

LOS 5e

40.   B

Month	Sales (xi)	Profit (yi)	$(x_i - \bar{x})$	$(y_i - \bar{y})$	$(x_i - \bar{x})(y_i - \bar{y})$
Jan	1,000	165	−500	−85	42,500
Feb	1,300	215	−200	−35	7,000
Mar	1,700	270	200	20	4,000
Apr	2,000	350	500	100	50,000
					103,500

Average of sales $\bar{X} = \dfrac{1000 + 1300 + 1700 + 2000}{4} = \dfrac{6000}{4} = 1,500$

Average of profit $\bar{y} = \dfrac{165 + 215 + 270 + 350}{4} = \dfrac{1000}{4} = 250$

Covariance $= \dfrac{\sum\limits_{i=1}^{n}(x_i - \bar{x})(y_i - \bar{y})}{n-1} = \dfrac{103,500}{3} = 34,500$

LOS 8k

41.   C   With a Normal distribution, 95 percent of the values occur within plus or minus two standard deviations of the mean.

Confidence interval= 100 ± 2(10)

= 80 to 120

LOS 9l

42.   B   Period 1: Beginning market value is $400,000. Ending market value plus dividends is $410,000.

Period 2: Beginning value is $390,000. Ending market value plus dividends is $430,000.

Period 1 return $= \dfrac{410,000 - 400,000}{400,000} = 0.02500$

Period 2 return $= \dfrac{430,000 - 390,000}{390,000} = 0.10256$

Time weighted return: $(1 + 0.025)(1 + 0.10256)^{0.5} - 1 = 0.063$ or 6.3%.

LOS 6d

43. **C** The mode by definition must be an observed value. It will not be distorted by extreme (infrequent) values.

LOS 7e

44. **B** 1 – probability of a Type II error = 1-0.2 = 0.8

LOS 11b and 11c

45. **B** According to Chebyshev's inequality, at least $1-\dfrac{1}{k^2}$ of values will lie within k standard deviations of the mean. At least 75% of observations lie within 2 standard deviations of the mean, i.e. $120 \pm 2 \times \sqrt{100}$, i.e. from 100 to 140.

LOS 7h

46. **C** The put/call ratio shows the proportion of the market buying downside protection (put options). Bollinger bands show price movements and the Stochastic oscillator shows the strength of trends.

LOS 12e

47. **C** I The sum of the probabilities of mutually exclusive and exhaustive events comes to 1.

   II If there is an unweighted dice, the probabilities can be worked out from logic (a priori) without the need to measure actual outcomes (empirical).

LOS 8a and 8b

48. **A** A larger sample size reduces the standard error which increases the test statistic.

LOS 10k

49. **C** p (more than six pass) = p (7 will pass) + p (8 will pass)
Using binomial theory:
p (pass) = 0.7
p (7 will pass) = $_8C_7 \times 0.7^7 \times 0.3^1 = 0.198$
p (8 will pass) = $_8C_8 \times 0.7^8 \times 0.3^0 = 0.0576$
p (more than six pass) = p (7 will pass) + p (8 will pass)
p (more than six pass) = 0.198 + 0.0576 = 0.256

LOS 8f

50. **A** Nominal scales categorize but do not rank. Interval scales are where the differences between scale values are equal.

LOS 7a

51. **A** $\dfrac{4}{\dfrac{1}{2}+\dfrac{1}{4}+\dfrac{1}{5}+\dfrac{1}{7}} = 3.7$

LOS 7e

52. **C** Since $\overline{X}$ must be farther than 2.33 standard errors from the mean for a one-tailed test to reject the null hypothesis, C is the only possible correct answer.

LOS 11c

53. **B** The distribution is less peaked and has smaller tails than a normal distribution (which reduces the value of its kurtosis).

LOS 7l

54. **B** A tree diagram:

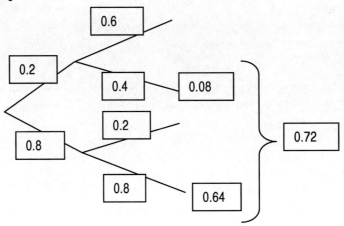

The upward branches indicate the credit rating rising to or staying at AAA. The downward branches represent it falling below or staying below AAA.

Without using a tree: $0.2 \times 0.4 + 0.8 \times 0.8 = 0.72$.

LOS 8d,f,j

55. **B** It is bounded by zero on the left and it has a long tail to the right.

LOS 9o

56. **B** When the population variance is known and the population is normally distributed, the sampling distribution of sample means will be normal, regardless of the sample size. In the other two cases, the population variance is unknown, so the appropriate distribution to use is the Student t distribution. Where the sample size is sufficiently large, this will approach a normal distribution.

LOS 10i,j

57. **C** It is important that the hypothesis can be disproved, otherwise there is no point in doing any hypothesis testing to try and disprove it.

LOS 11a

Equity

58. **A** A high rate of return attracts savers and discourages borrowers, so there will be more savers than borrowers. This will cause the rate to fall to its equilibrium level where savers equal borrowers.

   LOS 46a

59. **B** Preferred stock do not typically have voting rights and have a fixed interest in the assets of the company, usually based on their face value.

   LOS 46c

60. **C** The leverage factor is $\dfrac{1}{0.2} = 5$. The profits will be $5 \times 50\% = 250\%$.

   LOS 46f

61. **B** Fundamental weighting addresses this disadvantage of market capitalization index by using company size measures that are not determined by its price. The main disadvantage of an equal weighting index is that when prices move, the index needs rebalancing.

   LOS 47d

62. **B** $100 \times 52 + 250 \times 51 = \$17,950$

   LOS 46h

63. **C** A continuous market allows for continuous trading. It may be a dealer market or an auction market.

   LOS 46j

64. **B** For both price and market value weighted indexes, changes in stock price do not trigger a need to rebalance.

   LOS 47f

65. **B** Any restrictions on trading, such as high costs, lack of arbitrageurs to exploit inefficiencies, lack of short selling, will impede market efficiency.

   LOS 48c

66. **A** The semi-strong and strong forms state that all public information (which includes price to book ratios) is reflected in prices, meaning that it is not possible to use such information to make supernormal profits.

   LOS 48d,e

67. **C** The January anomaly suggests that investors sell stocks in December for tax reasons and then repurchase them in January. This depresses prices in December and increases prices in January, meaning that other investors should buy stocks in December and sell them in January.

   LOS 48f

68.　A　The higher risk of equities means that they earn a return premium and gives them more volatile returns over time.

LOS 49b

69.　A　There will be a difference between different classes of common share, but the difference depends on the company concerned.

LOS 49b

70.　B　Convertible preference shares can be converted into common stock. Participating preference shares receive a variable dividend in addition to their fixed dividend. Cumulative preference shares have no dividend rights that are similar to common stock.

LOS 49b

71.　A　Level I sponsored ADRs cannot be traded on exchanges, only the OTC market. As a result, registration requirements for the company concerned are more relaxed and there are no size limits imposed.

LOS 49d

72.　A　Increasing stockholders equity with an equity issue will automatically increase total book value. However, the impact on price per share is uncertain, as it depends on how management uses the money raised.

LOS 49g

73.　B　Companies in the same group should be similar to each other but different from companies in other groups. Hence the groups should be different from each other.

LOS 50b

74.　A　Low barriers to exit will reduce price based competition when there is excess capacity as some companies may leave the industry. Low customer bargaining power will increase the industry's pricing power. Higher pricing power should lead to higher return on invested capital.

LOS 50h

75.　B　$$\frac{2.00}{1.09} + \frac{2.10}{1.09^2} + \frac{2.30}{1.09^3} + \frac{27.00}{1.09^3} = 26.23$$

LOS 51d

76.　C　The high level of intangible assets makes the asset based approach difficult to apply. The company is not currently paying dividends, so it is most appropriate to focus on dividend paying capacity in the future.

LOS 51k

77.　C　Since the investment horizon should not affect the future cash flows/dividends or the discount rate, it will have no impact on value.

LOS 51e

78.   C $\dfrac{D_0(1+g)}{r-g} = \dfrac{10 \times 1.02}{0.07 - 0.02} = 204$

   LOS 51e

Financial Statement Analysis

79. **A**   The other options will not change the top or bottom of the current ratio as they simply move value between current assets. Paying off accounts receivable will reduce the top and bottom of the current ratio by the same amount which will increase the value. Try this with dummy numbers, e.g. reducing the top and bottom by 0.5 leads to a new current ratio of 1.2/0.5 = 2.4.

        LOS 28b

80. **A**   FIFO charges the earliest purchases to cost of goods sold and includes the later purchases in inventories. In times of rising prices it will give lower cost of goods sold (therefore higher gross profit) and higher inventory values as a result.

        LOS 29e

81. **B**   Capitalization of interest increases assets and since the interest is not treated as an expense against income, there will also be higher equity.

        LOS 30a

82. **C**   They are split into interest (operating cash flow) and capital (financing cash flow).

        LOS 32i

83. **C**   Depreciation method does not affect cash flow.

        LOS 30c

84. **B** $\text{Depreciation charge} = \dfrac{\text{NBV}}{\text{remaning life}} = \dfrac{(100-35)}{13} = \$5,000$

        LOS 30d

85. **C**

Earnings before interest and tax	10,000
Add Depreciation	1,000
Add loss on disposal of fixed asset	50
Change in accounts receivable (280-300)	(20)
Change in accounts payable (600-550)	50
Change in inventories (200 – 100)	100
Interest paid	(2,000)
Less tax (30% × 8000)	(2,400)
Cash flow from operations	6,780

        LOS 27a

86.   **A**

Cash flow from financing
Shares issued	3,000
Debt repaid	(700)
Dividend paid	(200)
CFF	2,100

LOS 27a

87.   **A**   A finance lease will give current and long term liabilities, being the PV of future lease payments. Current asset will be the same, a finance lease 'asset' will be shown in long term assets. Leases have no impact on cost of sale.

LOS 32h

88.   **C**   Straight-line will give a higher value for assets and less depreciation expense, hence, higher retained earnings. Total asset turnover will be lower because of the increased total asset value. Depreciation policy does not impact upon cash flows.

LOS 30c

89.   **A**   FIFO means cheaper stock is expended through cost of sales and the more expensive inventory remaining will give *higher* closing inventory valuation than LIFO.

LOS 29e

90.   **C**   The effective interest expense affects the income statement, not the cash flow statement. All cash flows are financing cash flows, therefore the operating cash flow will be overstated because there is no overall effect and no interest has been paid.

See LOS 32b

91.   **B** $80,000 ÷ nine years. Capitalize the asset at the lower of the PV of the minimum lease payments to be made and the fair value of the asset concerned. Depreciate the asset over the period of time that we receive the benefit of the lease.

LOS 32h

92.   **C**   ROE = Net margin × Asset turnover × Financial leverage

22.5 = 5 × 3 × Financial leverage

$$FL = \frac{22.5}{5 \times 3} = 1.5$$

LOS 28d

93.   **A**   The tax burden is 1-t, which means that the tax rate has moved from 30% to 35%. This will reduce net income so will definitely reduce ROE. The return on assets will help ROE and the impact of changing total assets is uncertain.

LOS 28d

94.   **C**   Realised exchange gains on purchases will be credited directly to the income statement and will appear within retained earnings in owners' equity but not as a separate line item.

LOS 26f

95. B There is no deferred tax impact associated with the exercise of stock options. There is a tax benefit when options are exercised in the period. This is usually disclosed within cash from operations.

LOS 34a

96. C

Opening NBV	1,000
+ Expenditure	500
– Depreciation (missing figure)	(280)
– NBV of assets sold (see below)	(20)
Closing NBV	1,200
Sale proceeds	50
NBV of asset sold (missing figure)	(20)
Profit on disposal	30

LOS 30d

97. C An increase in the valuation allowance will reduce the deferred tax asset and increase the tax expense in the income statement. Hence net income will fall and total asset turnover will increase. There will be no impact on cash flows.

LOS 31g

98. A A warning sign is when reported profits are high but operating cash flow is much lower – this could mean income is being booked early, before the cash comes in. The warning sign is that the cash flow earnings index is therefore consistently *below* 1.

LOS 33d

99. A Earnings

Net income $1.31m

Weighted Average Number of Shares

$$1/1/11 - 1/4/11 \qquad 4,250,000 \times \frac{3}{12} \times \frac{5}{3} \qquad = 1,770,833$$

Issued $\qquad\qquad\qquad\underline{1,250,000}$

$$1/4/11 - 1/7/11 \qquad 5,500,000 \times \frac{9}{12} \times \frac{5}{3} \qquad = \underline{6,875,000}$$

$$8,645,833$$

Note the stock split is treated as if it was effective from the start of the year

$$EPS = \frac{\$1.31\,m}{8,645,833} = \$0.15$$

LOS 25g

100. B Deferred taxes are an accounting adjustment required when there are temporary differences in timing between tax rules and accounting rules for recognition of income and expenses.

LOS 31a

101. **A** Revise future depreciation expense is spread over the remaining depreciable value of the revised estimated useful life.

   LOS 25e

102. **C** Goodwill is an unidentifiable **in**tangible asset which is subject to an annual impairment review.

   LOS 30e

103. **B** However, discounted cash flows are used when working out the recoverable amount.

   LOS 30h

104. **C** The other two are both solvency ratios. Quick and current ratios reflect the company's liquidity position in that they look at short term assets and liabilities.

   LOS 28b

105. **B** The deferred tax asset is based on the taxable losses that are more likely than not to be realized. The deferred tax asset in the accounts is therefore $35,000 × 30% = $10,500.

   LOS 31d

106. **A** Double-declining results in the highest depreciation charge in year 1 and hence the lowest NBV of assets at the year end. This gives the highest asset turnover. The highest depreciation charge will give the lowest profit margin.

   LOS 30c

107. **C** Other things being equal, a fall in a liability is deducted from net income to give operating cash flow.

   See LOS 32a

108. **B** The write-down of assets indicates that the depreciation charge in prior years has been too low causing prior year income to be overstated. Income will be understated because of the charge.

   LOS 30h

109. **A** The highly profitable long-term contract, Contract A, should increase ROE, since we recognize its profit over time and not in one lump at the end of the contract. Contract B should decrease ROE, since we recognise losses as they are incurred.

   LOS 25b

110. **A** When receivables are securitised cash from operations is higher. Share buy backs impact cash flows from financing and only the tax benefits of the options exercised impact upon cash flow from operations. Curtailing financing of payables is likely to reduce cash flow from operations.

   LOS 34a

111. **B** The leased asset is capitalized on the balance sheet. The CFO will actually be higher as some of the lease payment is categorized as a financing outflow. CFI is not affected.

   LOS 32i

112. **B** Growth screens focus on selecting high-earnings-growth companies – i.e. EPS and ROA are relevant. Option B is a screen for selecting a *value* stock rather than a growth stock, since the screen selects companies with a lower P/E.

LOS 35d

113. **C** Closing inventory under will be higher than LIFO because inventory of the higher, more recent purchases will be left in stock. This will mean the current asset value will rise and therefore the current ratio will be higher.

Cost of sales under FIFO will be lower because the cheaper, earlier purchased inventory will be expensed in cost of sales as it is sold.

LOS 35e

114. **C** Under the accrual method, cash flows are recognized in the cash flow statement when they occur. Income reported is more indicative of a firm's current productivity and operating results rather than the total cash flows for the period. A cash expense (or receipt) is allocated to the period in which it is incurred rather than when it is paid.

LOS 25b

115. **C** Staff training is an operating expense. Delivery and testing of a machine are capitalised as they are necessary to get the machine ready for use.

LOS 30a

116. **C** A common-size income statement expresses individual components as a percentage of sales and balance sheets express components as a percentage of total assets. Because the financial statements are expressed as percentages of the relevant base, they do not ease calculation of financial ratios using account totals other than those of the base, or the calculations of ratios involving averages of accounts from one period end to the next period end.

LOS 28a

117. **C** It should only be used for long-term contracts where there is a contract for sale and estimates of costs and revenues are reasonably certain.

LOS 25b

118. **B** To bring operating leases on-balance sheet, the present value of the future lease payments are capitalised as an asset and a corresponding liability shown. Therefore the asset base will increase and asset turnover ratio will decrease. The operating lease rental payments will be removed and replaced with a depreciation charge on the asset and interest on the liability. Therefore interest paid will rise and interest coverage will decrease. The increase in debt on the balance sheet will increase financial leverage, not operating leverage.

LOS 35e

119. **A** Unearned revenue represents revenue that has been collected but under the accruals concept has not yet been earned. The revenue will be released into the income statement over time.

LOS 23d

120. **C** Cash is not impacted upon by the accruals concept. Shareholders' equity will be overstated because of the profit recognized too soon. Receivables will be overstated because turnover will be recognized too soon.

LOS 33b

BPP
LEARNING MEDIA